COURAGEOUS WOMAN

COURAGEOUS WOMAN

31 Day Faith Devotional

JOEL TUDMAN

FIRST PRINTING, 2017

ISBN 9780692937686

THENETCHURCH.TV
4301 NE 23RD STREET
OKLAHOMA CITY, OK 73121

COVER DESIGN BY; ERIC HELLOMS
LAYOUT DESIGN BY: CHRISTINA HICKS CREATIVE

THENETCHURCH.TV

TABLE OF CONTENTS

INTRODUCTION

Courage: the ability to do something that frightens oneself, strength in the face of pain.

"Have I not commanded you? Be strong and courageous. Do not be afraid; do not be discouraged, for the Lord your God will be with you wherever you go."

(Joshua 1:9, New International Version)

I was blessed and fortunate to be raised by a single, saved mother. She taught my two siblings along with myself everything we know and flow in today. She is an amazing woman just like you! I believe that the strongest and most courageous creation on earth is the woman. It takes courageous faith to have kids, raise kids, support your kids' extracurricular activities, work to feed your kids, and then find a way to do it every day without breaking from the arduous responsibilities daily! I hear a quiet powerful voice saying I have no kids. I say my sister, you are just as or more courageous! I see you having to fight the male dominating system in the work force along with its sexist landscape. I see you managing your life of independence: pumping your own gas, arranging your oil changes, loading and unloading, carrying your groceries into your own home, in charge of your own safety, and the list goes on. Woman you are courageous; that means you're brave, strong, and not deterred by danger or pain.

Psychologist **Dr. Melanie Greenberg** gave six attributes to courage in physiology today:

- Feeling fear yet choosing to act
- Following your heart
- Persevering in the face of adversity
- Standing up for what is right
- Expanding your horizons, letting go of the familiar
- Facing suffering with faith

Dr. Greenberg's six attributes show us the power behind courage. Ernest Hemingway said, "Courage is grace under pressure." Courageous woman, there's one thing I know you do well and that is flow well under pressure. Psychologically I like what Greenberg has to say about her 6 attributes, but biblically God supplies us with four assisted with power. God can transform your mind through the Word and give you power to execute in this world.

God gives Joshua four critical life supporting phrases:

- Be strong and courageous
- Don't be afraid
- Don't be discouraged
- I'm with you wherever you go

In Joshua, God commands him; he doesn't ask him to be strong and courageous. He's taking over a leadership role where the previous leader is known as the greatest ever! Walking in courage was expected of him and it's also expected of you. God expects you to go bravely into new dimensions in Him and new territories in your world. God told Joshua He was going to be with him wherever he went. Wherever you go, courageous woman, God says don't fear or be discouraged because He's with you. Whether you're going to college, going into a new career, or in a new relationship, He's with you. I want you to know personally that you are appreciated for all the loyalty that you gave away for free in exchange for pain in return. It takes courage to keep smiling when pain is saying cry and shut down. Not only are you a courageous woman, but you're a woman of faith!

A woman full of faith and courage is a woman that can't be stopped! This 31-day devotional is faith food to help boost you from No Faith to Courageous Faith!

> "For unto us was the gospel preached, as well as unto them: but the word preached did not profit them, not being mixed with faith in them that heard it."
>
> (Hebrews 4:2, King James Version)

Our obligation is to believe God's Word and mix the Word with Faith to get the God kind of results! The Bible says "Faith comes by hearing and hearing by the Word of God!" In this Hebrew text, there are two audiences: them and us! "Them" didn't mix their faith with the Word but they heard it! Courageous woman, you aren't a part of **"them,"** you are a part of the «us» crowd! Courage makes you lift up your head and walk tall among the giants.

When you walk in courage, you're walking with God everywhere you go with no fear and no discouragement about who you are. God didn't give the spirit of fear He gave you power! Courage is on you; so take it and recover everything the enemy took from you. Courage pushes you, where fear terrifies you. This devotional is not giving fear a platform. You already know what it feels like to deal with fear. These daily devotionals were written to boost your faith past any fear that may be lurking around. God isn't investing fear into you. The enemy wants to inject fear to change your belief system. Courageous woman, walk in faith and don't even acknowledge fear. Acknowledging fear gives the enemy a place to set up camp and keep you on the edge of almost. You were not designed to sit and wonder what life would be like if you would've just had the courage to do what God said you could. Put faith to work and let him handle the tough stuff! Live in faith, walk in faith, and see the supernatural on the regular in your life!

Three Women Of Courage You Should Study

In the scriptures, **Ester** walked tall and handled the pressure of her nation's existence with courageous faith. She saved her nation in faith. She was so courageous. She walked in to speak with the king without him extending his scepter. It was customary for the king to extend his scepter when someone in his presence wanted to speak. If the king didn't extend his scepter and they spoke anyway, that was grounds for execution. But she spoke anyway! She spoke in faith. She made a courageous move. She did what others feared to do. God was with her. Courageous woman, where would the world be without you? You have ability in you to do what has frightened others.

Look at **Mary,** the mother of Jesus. She risked everything to carry Jesus. She almost lost her fiancé carrying Jesus. She had to have courageous faith to even believe the spirit had impregnated her. She was courageous!

Look at **Debra** in the Old Testament. She was a wife, a renowned prophetess, honored judge, and the ideal woman called to lead. She was the only female judge and the only one that walked in the prophetic. She kept it clear that her Lord was in charge. She was fearless and courageous!

There are many other women in the Bible that were courageous and those of you who are reading this are full of courageous faith now! "Be alert. Continue strong in the faith. Have courage, and be strong." (1 Corinthians 16:13, New Century Version)

Father, thank you for giving me the supernatural courage to go forward. As I read this 31-day devotional, I believe my measure of faith is going to increase. I am courageous in Jesus' name. Amen.

Day 1

A mind that meditates will
turn into a life that manifest.

COURAGEOUS MEDITATION

"This book of the law shall not depart out of thy mouth; but thou shalt meditate therein day and night, that thou mayest observe to do according to all that is written therein: for then thou shalt make thy way prosperous, and then thou shalt have good success."
(Joshua 1:8, King James Version)

Mediation is the filling of the mind, to utter, mutter, speak out loud, groan, ponder or rehearse in one›s mind.

Meditation is not a new move of God and it isn't some new practice. He put it in His Word for us to have success. It is His way for good success. Meditation is not daydreaming. It is conscious thought control—on the Word of God. When you fill your mind with the Word, you have a faith fighting chance to be word influenced. The word fill means to have an overwhelming presence in. The Word of God has to have an overwhelming presence in you. It has everything you need for you to make your way successful.

Make sure you observe to do the Word that you're putting in your mouth. Act on it! When you act on something, you prove that you really believe it! This all prospers you by God's design and destines you for good success. Success is tied to you, woman of God.

"Through faith we understand that the worlds were framed by the word of God, so that things which are seen were not made of things which do appear."

(Hebrews 11:3, King James Version)

Your words can frame your tomorrow. They can frame your future by building foundations, creating borders, and setting boundaries. Frame your today and your tomorrow with God's Word. His word has been used to do it before, and the last time I checked he's the same yesterday, today, and forevermore.

Courageous woman, stay in command of your life and keep filling your mind with the Word. Though the mind is a busy place, muttering God's Word will help you keep it clear. As you meditate, you are filling the mind with God's Word, God's Way, and God's Act.

- **Word** - His Instruction
- **Way** - His Direction
- **Acts** - His Action

Believe on what you meditate. Read his instructions, trust and follow his direction, believe that his actions can happen for you. While you're meditating on Him, He will be ministering to you.

"For the Word that God speaks is alive and full of power [making it active, operative, energizing, and effective]; it is sharper than any two-edged sword, penetrating to the dividing line of the breath of life (soul) and [the immortal] spirit, and [of joints and marrow of the deepest parts of our nature], exposing and sifting and analyzing and judging the very thoughts and purposes of the heart." (Hebrews 4:12, Amplified Bible, Classic Edition)

The Word that you're meditating on is alive and breathing. It is protecting you from your own nature. Meditate on it...

Here's five simple ways to meditate on God's Word today:
- Study the Word
- Speak the Word out loud
- Imagine what the Word says you are
- Utter and Mutter the Word
- Listen to the Word

Joshua tells us to meditate day and night—a continuous practice that will make you prosperous. Remember a mind that meditates will turn into a life that manifests.

Father, thank you for your Word that provides me with your ways, directions, and actions. I will meditate on your word constantly and keep it in my mouth. In Jesus' name. Amen.

Day 2

Your heart is the driving force of motivation and as you sow thoughts of pursuit, you will become what you think.

COURAGEOUS PURSUIT

"I'm single-minded in pursuit of you; don't let me miss the road signs you've posted."

(Psalm 119:10, The Message)

Pursue: seek to attain or accomplish
Single-minded: concentration on one aim or purpose

Go—such a simple command! I'm telling you it's time go and get what you've dreamed of and prayed for! Go in faith, and stay in faith as you go! Pursuit of your goals reveal your faith in your go. Courageous faith pursues period. If it's not pursuing physically, it's pursuing strategically or mentally. So a woman thinks in her heart, so is she. Your heart is the driving force of motivation and as you sow thoughts of pursuit, you will become what you think. Courageous pursuit involves both your motor and mental abilities. Moving mentality is hardly ever the issue. Mental imaging and thinking while being under pressure can cloud the motivation to move physically. Stay in hot pursuit of your dreams regardless of the attacks you're encountering.

GO Courageous Woman

This key verse says to be **single-minded**—one aim or one purpose that becomes your concentration. Find a Word for what you're pursuing, put your faith to work, be courageous, and concentrate. Concentration is the power of a focused mind. You are a product of your concentration. Your courageous pursuit is powerful and it can't be accomplished without faith in extreme situations. Go, and go knowing God has already placed signs for you along the way. Road signs can't be viewed from your bed at home. You must hit the road first and see second. The Word says that we walk by faith and not by sight. This doesn't mean we're blind. It means our pursuits aren't hindered by what we do and don't see. We see what the Word says regardless what our eyes show. This is why we have to remain single-minded, because our natural will try to talk us out of tough pursuits.

In this verse, the psalmist describes the pursuit of God and how your mind needs to be, to keep from missing what He's posted for you to see. What God has to show you will require your discernment. You've missed enough already, so meditate and concentrate. Keep the courage and go believing what His word says about his posted sign on your path.

Psalms 119:10 can be used to describe your pursuit of anything you want to accomplish! Go knowing. Go with courageous faith and attain, accomplish, and even discover more.

Father, thank you for the victory signs you've posted just for me out in front of me. I have the courage to go knowing without having to physically see. In Jesus' name. Amen.

Day 3

Courageous women are courageous overcomers, and they aren't struggling to come through, they walk through.

COURAGEOUS OVERCOMER

"Every God-begotten person conquers the world's ways. The conquering power that brings the world to its knees is our faith. The person who wins out over the world's ways is simply the one who believes Jesus is the Son of God."

(1 John 5:4-5, The Message)

Overcomer: a person who prevails over opposition, temptation, weakness and establishes ascendancy.

Ascendancy: a position of dominant power

When you were born again, The Overcomer took up residence in your spirit. Conquering power is flowing in you now, as we speak. Romans 8:37 says you are more than a conqueror through him that loves you. The days of being defeated and down have been dismissed. If God be for you who can be against you? Woman of God, you're seated in heavenly places now at the right hand of the Father. See all trials and tribulations from heaven's seat and not your earthly seat. A major mistake people often make when speaking of being an overcomer is strengthening the trial or tribulation trying them. This minimizes who you are while walking through the shadows of darkness. Use your courageous faith and say who He says you are while you're in the trying moment. You are still above, the head, the lender, redeemed, saved, chosen, royal, blessed, friend of God, fearfully and wonderfully made, his treasured possession, and so much more. Today, realize your conquering power will bring any battle to its knees through your courageous faith. Say to yourself, right now, **I am a believer; I belong to God**.

I love the way The Message translates 1 John 4:4:

"My dear children, you come from God and belong to God. You have already won a big victory over those false teachers, for the Spirit in you is far stronger than anything in the world."

Courageous woman, God called you an overcomer and that alone should charge your faith! You are God-begotten, which simply means you are of God! You're not an overcomer because of what you've done mentally and emotionally to get over *it*, you were an overcomer before you went through *it*. You are of God! You have already won a big victory. Stop listening to what the world is saying about what you are dealing with. It's not denial, it's God-dependence. Glory to God! The Spirit in you is stronger than anything in the world. Courageous women are courageous overcomers and they aren't struggling to come through, they walk through. Courageous faith is in command; you have more power than you've been using. *The person who wins out over the world's ways is simply the one who believes Jesus.* You're not just an overcomer you're in power!

Thank you, father, for the overcoming power you placed in me prior to trials and tribulations. I have a power stronger in me than anything in the world! I was born to overcome everything the enemy throws at me. I win in Jesus' name. Amen.

Day 4
The level of your choices are about to upgrade.

COURAGEOUS CHOICES

"A man's mind plans his way, but the Lord directs his steps and makes them sure."

(Proverbs 16:9, Amplified Bible, Classic Edition)

Choice: the act of selecting when there are two or more possibilities

Life without choice is a life many people have lived and a life many are living now, because their freedom has been lost and or seized. It is an absolute blessing to have the freedom to choose, but it's a travesty when you're free to choose and you won't. Choice begins in the mind and is decided mentally before the tongue and mouth gives it a voice. There are people who are living with multiple choices but can't verbalize them, because they're paralyzed with the fear of making the wrong decision or they won't do the due diligence to choose rightly.

Courageous faith doesn't freeze in the face of options and neither is it chained having lost its freedom to choose. Courageous woman, you were designed to have choices and the spirit of fear is dominated by your design.

"God didn't give you the spirit of fear; but of power and love and a sound mind." (2 Timothy 1:7)

God made you and gave you dominion over the Earth. Eve had choices in the garden and her choices were among the best of everything God made for them! Can I tell you the level of your choices are about to upgrade? You will begin to choose from better selections. No more having to choose from what you had to settle with. Those days are over! Courageous woman, you can choose the best of houses, cars, restaurants, hotels, clothes, schools, jobs, cities to live in, etc.

Choose from the best, but have the courage to do two things:

- Make a Choice.
- Choose to follow God's direction even when it doesn't match your choice.

Courageous faith moves toward God, because the courage to follow comes from the Word. Faith comes by hearing the Word and the Word is where the directions come from. The Lord is directing and will make you sure of it, so leave Him in it and don't take him out of it! This verse shows us how you can make your plans but God can direct you from what you've planned. Will you choose His steps over your plans? Trust him, courageous woman.

Remember this proverb:

"When you walk, you won't be held back; when you run, you won't stumble." **(Proverbs 4:12, New Living Translation)**

Dear Lord, I thank you for direction and I choose to follow your option over mine. In Jesus' name. Amen.

Day 5
Your shameless, courageous, persistent action
has to correspond with your believing...

COURAGEOUS ACTION

"And I say unto you, Ask, and it shall be given you; seek, and ye shall find; knock, and it shall be opened unto you."

(Luke 11:9, King James Version)

Action: the process of doing something; a thing done.

It's time for you to take action and not just the typical action that you've been taking. Courageous woman, I'm talking about action that requires you to have faith in your faith. You have ideas and plans that need more than your intellect and connections. Your shameless, courageous, persistent action has to correspond with your believing if you're going to receive what you want from God. No more of just being a hearer of God's Word; you are going to have to do it to possess it.

"But don't just listen to God's word. You must do what it says. Otherwise, you are only fooling yourselves. For if you listen to the word and don't obey, it is like glancing at your face in a mirror.

You see yourself, walk away, and forget what you look like. But if you look carefully into the perfect law that sets you free, and if you do what it says and don't forget what you heard, then God will bless you for doing it." (James 1:22-25, New Living Translation)

Self-deception is the manifestation of a hearer that won't do what he hears in the Word. Courageous woman, if you're not acting, you're not believing. The enemy wants you to believe in your head and never trust to move with your feet. God is going to bless you if you're following the Word. Our key verse, Matthew 7:7, says: "Ask, and it shall be given you; seek, and ye shall find; knock, and it shall be opened unto you." I don't know if the next move you want to make is big or small, but I can tell you this: your participation is needed. You're not in the wish business, you're in the faith business!

"For everyone who asks and keeps on asking receives; and he who seeks and keeps on seeking finds; and to him who knocks and keeps on knocking, the door shall be opened." (Luke 11:10, Amplified Bible)

Your continuing action is the proof you believe. Action can't stop because you don't feel like you're getting anywhere. You must live by faith and that means having faith every day. Faith is action. You are not trying to believe, you are believing.

Dear Lord, I will not be ashamed to ask, seek, or knock my way into destiny. My actions are in faith, by faith, and through faith! I am courageous! Amen.

Day 6

A courageous woman isn't a worn out woman.
She's courageous enough to say No and Re Up to
be a Yes that's dependable.

COURAGEOUS ME TIME

"The apostles sent out as missionaries came back and gathered together to Jesus, and told Him all that they had done and taught. [31] And He said to them, As for you come away by yourselves to a deserted place, and rest a while--for many were continually coming and going, and they had not even leisure enough to eat. [32] And they went away in a boat to a solitary place by themselves."

(Mark 6:30-32, Amplified Bible)

Me Time: we're not speaking of selfishness, but merely resting and refreshing

Take some time for yourself. You deserve some relaxation and you're going to have to be courageous enough to put yourself first today. Yes, people matter and you are a servant; however, you were not designed to function from the anointing only. The anointing comes upon you to complete a task and operate, but your body was given to you by God to take care of. You must steward it well. Jesus said the spirit of God was upon him to do various things. He had to take care of His body in order to be used the way the Father used him. Take care of your body, mind, and emotions so the Spirit can continue to come upon you. It's time to refresh your body and mind so you can expand beyond your current capacity and be more effective than you've ever been. When I say me time, I'm not talking about abandoning responsibilities; I'm merely saying rest yourself. I've watched many women care and care and care for others and take no time for themselves. You are a spirit that lives in a body and that body needs rest, exercise, sleep, fun and some sun. Take some time for you! God rested from creating the world. Adam was resting while Eve was being fashioned. Jesus, himself, often withdrew to pray and refocus (see Luke 5:16). One version says he retired into the wilderness to pray. He did this often—to be filled up in order to release grace back to the people!

Our key verse shows Jesus instructing his disciples to rest. There was a lot of going and coming. I'm sure you can understand this description of life. They had been serving others so much that they hadn't even eaten lunch so he tells them to come with him! Ladies, they got on a boat and went to a solitary place with Jesus! This is real rest and real me time! You are not letting anyone down by building yourself up, so use the same courageous faith you've been using for healing, money, marriage matters, and business deals for your health and wellness! A courageous woman isn't a worn out woman, she's courageous enough to say no and re-up to be a yes that's dependable. Stay courageous!

Six Tips For Your Time

1. Jesus says it's ok.
2. He's going with you.

3. Tell him on the way about your service.
4. Rest while you are there.
5. It's okay to rest in style (boat).
6. If everyone knows where you're going, you might as well stay where you are!

(Inform those that need to know and go)

Father, thank you for rest, relaxation, and refreshing. I thank you for tending to me. In Jesus' name. Amen!

Day 7

Forgiveness isn't about a moment to tell someone
I forgive you, it is the display of the abundant life
that Jesus gave to us.

COURAGEOUS FORGIVENESS

"Make allowance for each other's faults, and forgive anyone who offends you. Remember, the Lord forgave you, so you must forgive others."

(Colossians 3:13 New Living Translation)

Forgiveness: the action of forgiving which is to stop feeling angry and resentful toward an offense, flaw, mistake or even something done intentionally.

To forgive is all about a particular moment of choice that manifests from the position of your inner man. When I say inner man, I'm speaking of your spiritual condition. We preach about forgiving, but in reality we should be living a life of forgiveness. What I mean is live with an awareness that we've been forgiven and live to forgive to perpetuate this lifestyle. Forgiveness isn't about a moment to tell someone I forgive you. It is the display of the abundant life that Jesus gave to us. He walked in forgiveness. He forgave everyone.

He forgave those that the people wanted to kill in scripture. He forgave you. Forgive us of our trespasses as we forgive those who trespass against us. This is what He taught the disciples when they asked Him to teach them how to pray. Even our prayer lives are fitted with forgiveness.

Forgiveness is a cycle that the enemy wants to break so hatred and anger can run loose on the Earth. This is where your courageous faith kicks in! Woman of God, forgiveness helps you more than it does your offender. It frees you of the emotional torment and keeps you from caging yourself in with the invisible bars of isolation. Those days are over! No more walking around bundled up with bitterness. Free yourself of the toxic deposits of not forgiving someone produces. It takes a lot to forgive, but it takes courageous faith to live it. Staying conscious of what Jesus has done for you will feed your faith. Find all the scriptures on forgiveness, write them, memorize some of them, and your faith will grow in this area. Our key verse says we are to make allowance for each other's faults. Know that offense will happen and look for the opportunity to show mercy, forgive, and keep the cycle of this graceful forgiveness flowing! You are a courageous woman with courageous faith that's full of forgiveness. The Lord forgave you, so you must forgive others.

<u>Remember:</u>
Act in faith and forgive now.
Call or do it face to face.
Forgiveness isn't an option, it's a mandate.
Forgiveness is spiritual.

Lord, thank you for the grace you've given me. I now move in this same grace to forgive those who have wronged me! I move in faith courageously now. In Jesus' name. Amen.

Day 8
The life God has for you is too blessed for bad
memories to block you.

COURAGEOUS
MEMORY/FORGETTING

"Then he says, 'I will never again remember their sins and lawless deeds.'"

(Hebrews 10:17, New Living Translation)

Forgetting: putting something out of your mind by ceasing to think of it.

Forgetting is a subject many will have different opinions on, because so many have disappointing experiences. Satan uses people to do some really hurtful things. If we're not careful and prayerful we can find ourselves fueled with bitterness from constant images of deceit in our mind. You are probably saying I'm not God, pastor, and I can't just forget what people have done to me. You are correct in one aspect: you are not God. I'm telling you that if you can easily forget the good God has done, not give him the credit he deserves, and the good others have done, then you can forget the evil others have done. I know there are many extreme cases of pure evil people have done to many of you reading this right now.

Paul says , "Brothers, I do not consider that I have made it my own. But one thing I do: forgetting what lies behind and straining forward to what lies ahead." (Philippians 3:13, English Standard Version) What was done lies behind you. The more you continue to ponder about what has happened the longer it will take for you to forget it. Forgetting, sitting, re-thinking doesn't help you. People often can't forget certain memories because of the feelings attached to them. This is why it takes courageous faith to move forward. Faith is a higher power than your senses so advice in this area will have to come from people of faith. Put your faith to work and your faith will operate independently of your senses. I know you're saying I hear you but, that's not forgetting. Use this Hebrew scripture as a faith builder. If it's in His Word you can have it in your life. God forgets and you can, too, because you are a child of God! It's in your inherited devine nature. You are a new creature and the old has passed away! Don't put restrictions on the word just keep saying and believing it. Receive the newness and replace old images in your mind with new ones from His Word. Nothing is impossible to him that believes.

The life God has for you is too blessed for bad memories to block you. People will have to remind you by retelling the horror stories over and over for you to even recall of what they're speaking. God is going to bless you in such a way that the good will outweigh the bad. What he has for you is beyond wonderful, so receive it and walk in it courageously. Your memory is blessed!

God is about to fill your mind with new blessings in such a way He's forgotten some of the good stuff he's already done, as well.

"But forget all that- it is nothing compared to what I am going to do. [19] For I am about to do something new. See, I have already begun!

Do you not see it? I will make a pathway through the wilderness. I will create rivers in the dry wasteland." (Isaiah 43:18-19, New Living Translation)

Some people want you to remember so you can talk about it. Forget it all. Nope not interested! I'm moving forward to what lies ahead.

Lord, I have the courage to move on with a new mind that's ready for new memories! I can't perceive the new when all I think about is the old! I'm forgetting as I speak and seeing the new with the eyes of my courageous faith. In Jesus' name. Amen.

Day 9

Don't put limitations on your desires.
God's supply is bigger than they are.

COURAGEOUS DESIRES

"Take delight in the LORD, and he will give you your heart's desires."

(Psalm 37:4, New Living Translation)

Desires: strong feeling of wanting something.

Well, bless God, courageous woman! You serve a God who will supply your needs and give you your heart's desires. If you have the courage to believe for it he has the power the supply it. Don't put limitations on your desires; God's supply is bigger than your desires. There are many reasons people place limitations on their desires, but those days, for you, are over. Don't be moved by the conversations of those who are disgusted with God because they haven't received their desires. Do not change your belief. You stay in the Word and act on what it says. You can pray for your desires, but what good is praying if you don't believe. You have to believe God will do what you've asked.

"So I tell you to believe that you have received the things you ask for in prayer, and God will give them to you." (Mark 11:24, New Century Version)

If you notice, this verse clearly says believe you have received. That is past tense. Receive it in faith before you ever see it in the natural! This is courageous faith! So, believe you have it before you ask for it and he will give it to you. You can question it all you want, but until you follow it you will always be out of faith. Get faith and get your desires.

Take Delight In Him

Taking delight in the Lord changes everything because you make Him first instead of your wish list. Placing Him first changes you and it changes the natural order of asking and receiving. Normally people live for things, look for people to give them things, or set their desires on things. For the believers, it is the exact opposite. We set our desires on Him and seek him first. As you seek Him first He will add things to your life.

"But more than anything else, put God's work first and do what He wants. Then the other things will be yours as well." (Matthew 6:33, Contemporary English Version)

The promise He gives us in his word says that He will add things to us if we seek Him first! Seek means to desire to obtain. Your desire to please Him should be stronger than your desire of a husband, business, or financial increase. Take delight in Him.

Delighting in anything is all about pleasure. It is enjoyment! You should enjoy Him being first place in your life and have reverential fear for Him. Living in the fear of God isn't being afraid of God it's honoring Him. Honoring God comes with great benefits.

"Bless (affectionately, gratefully praise) the Lord, O my soul; and all that is [deepest] within me, bless His holy name!" (Psalm 103:2, Amplified Bible, Classic Edition)

As you delight in Him, you will love and want to please Him. He becomes the center of your joy and you live to commune with him. We all have desires, but for God to honor and supply them they can't be undisciplined desires; in other words, desires gone wild. Courageous woman, God wants to give you the desires of a heart that belongs to Him.

He Will Give You Your Hearts Desires

God is going to give you your heart's desires. He will freely transfer possessions to you. Your delivered desires from God are a product of heaven—you seeking Him, not the idea of you seeking Him. If you seek Him with your whole heart it will be changed, and He will give your heart its desires. Courageous woman, you won't have to compromise yourself for anyone to receive the desires of your heart, because your heart belongs to God and He's got you! Keep the faith and delight in Him, and the rest will take care of its self!

Father, I thank you for directing my desires and providing me with those desires! **Psalm 20:4 (New Living Translation) says,** "You grant my heart's desires and make all my plans succeed." In Jesus' name, I receive. Amen.

Day 10

You need a standard to measure yourself by,
or you will rob yourself and your neighbor of
the love that's available and deserving.

COURAGEOUS LOVE I

"The second is equally important: 'Love your neighbor as yourself.' No other commandment is greater than these."

(Mark 12:31, New Living Translation)

Love: the Word clearly defines it in Corinthians.

"Love is patient and kind. Love is not jealous or boastful or proud [5] or rude. It does not demand its own way. It is not irritable, and it keeps no record of being wronged. [6] It does not rejoice about injustice but rejoices whenever the truth wins out. [7] Love never gives up, never loses faith, is always hopeful, and endures through every circumstance."

(1 Corinthians 13:4-7, New Living Translation)

We know God is Love, that He loves us. We are to love Him in return, love our neighbors, and—the command we tend to overlook—love ourselves. What is loving yourself? Loving yourself is not a sin nor is it selfishness. It is actually the basis on which you're able to love your neighbors. Mark is simply saying love others the way you love yourself. Courageous woman, are you loving yourself? If you're churchy, you've got the hug and smile down to a T when it comes to loving others, but that is only a display and not necessarily a display of love for others. Do you love yourself?

Here's an easy way to find out courageous woman:
- Are you patient with yourself?
- Are you boastful, proud, or rude?
- Do you demand your own way?
- Are you an irritable woman?
- Do you rejoice in the truth about yourself?
- Do you give up?
- Do you lose the faith?
- Do you endure through every situation?

These eight questions are simply the Word of God in Corinthians that define love. You need a standard to measure yourself by or you'll rob yourself and your neighbor of the love that's available and deserved. Be courageous enough to embrace the truth about yourself from the Word's perspective and love yourself God's way! You deserve your own love and you don't have to wait to be loved. God loves you and you can love yourself the way God says to love! Be courageous and love yourself! In 1 Corinthians 13:7, Paul says, "Love never gives up, never loses faith, is always hopeful, and endures through every circumstance."

Don't give up on yourself in any situation. God is with you and you are courageous! Love yourself through every circumstance.

Day 11

It's ok to be vulnerable and love others without
them showing any signs of loving you back.

COURAGEOUS LOVE II

"Beloved, let us love one another: for love is of God; and every one that loveth is born of God, and knoweth God."

(1 John 4:7, King James Version)

Love: the Word clearly defines it in Corinthians.

"Love is patient and kind. Love is not jealous or boastful or proud [5] or rude. It does not demand its own way. It is not irritable, and it keeps no record of being wronged. [6] It does not rejoice about injustice but rejoices whenever the truth wins out. [7] Love never gives up, never loses faith, is always hopeful, and endures through every circumstance."

(1 Corinthians 13:4-7, New Living Translation)

Courageous woman, because you know how to love yourself through anything you are poised to love others the same way. You have God's ability available in you to love others. God's love is alive within you now! Jesus explains to us that love is of God, so the more we love others the more of God is exposed through us. Love is of God and He is eternal, exceptional, omnipresent omniscient, omnipotent. That means the love you're displaying is everlasting, excellent, everywhere, knows everything and is all powerful. What a description of love! He's not asking you to do this on your own because you're not capable, but you can do all things through him. You can love all people!

Be courageous with your faith and love others with His influence. It's okay to be vulnerable and love others without them showing any signs of loving you back. Love draws people into the kingdom of God!

"The Lord appeared from of old to me [Israel], saying, Yes, I have loved you with an everlasting love; therefore with loving-kindness have I drawn you and continued My faithfulness to you." (Jeremiah 31:3, Amplified Bible, Classic Edition)

God's everlasting love is used to draw us into Him. He chooses to be faithful with His love. What a standard to put before our lives—a faithful love.

If you choose not to love, where is the love going to come from? Stop letting the others do the loving. No more relying on someone else to love while you sit back and just like them! Love and love hard. If for some reason you're hurt in the process, God's love is faithful to you. You're never without love because you're never without God! He said, "Lo I'll be with you even until the end!

Father, I thank you for your love. Teach me your ways of love that I may demonstrate the God kind of love in the Earth to cease the cycle of hatred and pseudo-love. In Jesus' name. Amen.

Day 12
Real love isn't concerned about
getting it in return.

COURAGEOUS LOVE III

"But I say unto you which hear, Love your enemies, do good to them which hate you,"

(Luke 6:27, King James Version)

Love: the Word clearly defines it in Corinthians.

"Love is patient and kind. Love is not jealous or boastful or proud [5] or rude. It does not demand its own way. It is not irritable, and it keeps no record of being wronged. [6] It does not rejoice about injustice but rejoices whenever the truth wins out. [7] Love never gives up, never loses faith, is always hopeful, and endures through every circumstance."

(1 Corinthians 13:4-7, New Living Translation)

Enemies are thorns in the flesh, especially if you love people and I believe you are a lover of people! It's really easy to love those who show love back, but it definitely takes courageous faith to love those you know don't like, can't stand, and even hate you! Well, guess what? God commands us to love our enemies and to love them no less than anyone else. Show them the God-kind of love and let them know you're incapable of being an enemy to them! You have too much of God's love in you to hate back!

"If you love only someone who loves you, will God praise you for that? Even sinners love people who love them. If you are kind only to someone who is kind to you, will God be pleased with you for that? Even sinners are kind to people who are kind to them. If you lend money only to someone you think will pay you back, will God be pleased with you for that? Even sinners lend to sinners because they think they will get it all back." (Luke 6:32-34, Contemporary English Version)

Real love isn't concerned about getting it in return. It knows its job is to fill the Earth with love so love will have a chance to change the world. Jesus opens our key verse saying, "I say unto you which hear." I believe this is the most critical portion of the verse. Courageous woman, will you allow yourself to hear this word? Faith only comes by hearing, and a lot of the reasons faith can't be found is because the Word won't be heard! Hear this: love your enemy not like them, ignore them, or feed them from a long-handled spoon. He says love them and do good to them that hate you. Love is action and if we truly love, we will have to demonstrate it to the forces that rise up against us. Do good, no matter what! Don't give the enemy the satisfaction of turning you from love into hate. Courageous woman, all Jesus is asking for you to do is go higher than the hatred of your enemy. You have God's ability.

Father, I thank you for the God-kind of love. I will love my enemies the way you said for me to love them. I won't forget that I once was an enemy of yours and you still loved me first! Thank you. In Jesus' name. Amen!

Day 13
Living in God's love is how your
courageous faith is fueled.

COURAGEOUS LOVE IV

"But God showed his great love for us by sending Christ to die for us while we were still sinners."

(Romans 5:8 New Living Translation)

Love: the Word clearly defines it in Corinthians.

"Love is patient and kind. Love is not jealous or boastful or proud [5] or rude. It does not demand its own way. It is not irritable, and it keeps no record of being wronged. [6] It does not rejoice about injustice but rejoices whenever the truth wins out. [7] Love never gives up, never loses faith, is always hopeful, and endures through every circumstance."

(1 Corinthians 13:4-7, New Living Translation)

God's love for you isn't determined by your goodness, your gifting, or your giving. God isn't in need of anything from you. You have to come into the knowledge of who He really is to you, what He's provided for you, and what He can do through you. Put your trust in

His love. If you live in Him you will live in love and God will live in you! Living in God's love is how your courageous faith is fueled.

"For when we place our faith in Christ Jesus, there is no benefit in being circumcised or being uncircumcised. What is important is faith expressing itself in love." **(Galatians 5:6, New Living Translation)**

"For in Jesus Christ neither circumcision availeth any thing, nor uncircumcision; but faith which worketh by love." **(Galatians 5:6, King James Version)**

Faith Works By Love

We have to get to know His love beyond knowledge far deep into experiencing him. He loves you—He hates sin—but He loves the sinner. He doesn't wait until you change to love you. He loves you hoping his goodness will draw you into repentance. **Romans 2:4**

It's not enough to talk about it; you need to experience His love. Sit and reflect on how His love has been with you through your good and bad. God's love is different than any man's love. Man is conditional in his love, where God is unconditional. With this type of love living in you it provides courageous power that allows you to love those who don't like you and/or mistreat you. Many people throw the **L** word around loosely. Today it is one of the most watered down words in people's vocabulary. I'm so glad God is not a man! He is God and He can't lie! If God said He loves you, it's the holy truth!

In our key verse, the Roman writer says, "God showed His great love." He didn't say He loved us, my sister, it said He showed His great love. He showed it by sending His son as our substitute. We should've been punished for our sins, but Jesus took our place on the cross. He died for us while we were still in our sin! Courageous woman, this is the kind of God you serve—one that loves first regardless! He gave his life for you.

"No one has greater love no one has shown stronger affection than to lay down (give up) his own life for his friends. Jesus goes on further to say you are his friend and not a slave. You are Gods friend. The moment you start to drift heavy into your emotions thinking God doesn't love you lean back on the Word; not your understanding. Remember you are a courageous woman with a powerful friend!" (John 15:13, Amplified Bible, Classic Edition)

Father, I thank you for showing your incredible unconditional love to me. I will let nothing separate me from your love. In Jesus' name. Amen.

Day 14
A transformed life is a changed life.

COURAGEOUS CHANGE

" And be not conformed to this world: but be ye transformed by
the renewing of your mind, that ye may prove what is that good,
and acceptable, and perfect, will of God."

(Romans 12:2, King James Version)

Change: to make or become different, an alteration or modification,
a new or refreshingly different experience, a substitute of one thing
for another.

Change isn't a stranger to anyone on this Earth. People evolve
over the years and adapt to change at different speeds. Preparing for
change is much easier than being surprised by change. When you
live forward, pay attention to trends in the world, and how things
shift change can be anticipated. The world uses social media and
television to tell its vision for anything it wants to change. It doesn't
get your permission, it seizes your attention and then it pinches you
into position. The kingdom casts vision to people, in order to keep

God's vision in the mind of its people. It's a war on change. The world wants you one way and the kingdom wants you in another.

Courageous woman, even your nature is being challenged in this era as to whether or not you are a wife or a husband. There is a battle going on and this world needs courageous women who aren't ashamed to be women of God.

Paul says, "Be not conformed to this world. Conformed means to comply with standards, rules, and laws." He's saying be Godly courageous and do not comply with what the world says but rather what God says.

Keep yourself constantly in books and involved in productive conversations and your mind will be prepared for change. Change is good and not always bad. Don't quit because of the threat of some backlash. I understand it can be quite frightening at times, but one truth that hasn't changed is Jesus. He's the same yesterday, today, and forever! His consistency is foundational and more than enough for you to build upon allowing yourself to go through changes with no sweat.

Let's face the truth, you might just need to change yourself. Sometimes we just have to look into the mirror of the Word and simply be honest with ourselves. Be courageous enough to embrace the changes that are needed—accept them and adapt to them! Don't conform to the world's way! A transformed life is a changed life. Change will start when you begin renewing your mind. The renewed mind is a new mind, a changed mind. As you continue to renew your mind, you and change will become one.

If the same thing keeps happening, a change needs to take place not another apology. Change and allow the Word to be the catalyst for that change. You're getting ready to prove what is good, acceptable, and the perfect will of God by using the Word as your source for change. Using any other information or person makes them the standard for change. The Word is your standard, not other's opinions or experiences.

Father, I thank you for the changes in me, around me, and those that are going to revolutionize me. In Jesus' name. Amen.

Day 15
To finish anything of any substance requires
discipline, denial, determination,
and discernment.

COURAGEOUS FINISHER

"Finishing is better than starting. Patience is better than pride."
(Ecclesiastes 7:8 New Living Translation)

Finisher: a person or thing that finishes something, to bring to a completion, the final part or the last stage.

Are you a finisher? I pray your answer is yes, because you should be. Paul, in his letter to the Philippians church, said, " I am confident that He who began a good work in you will bring it to completion at the day of Jesus Christ." God is the He he's referring to, and He is a finisher! You were born of Him and born again to finish what you start. Rest in Jesus' finished work and obey His way into completion. It was on the cross of Calvary where He stayed and said "It is finished." He could've left the cross at any time but He finished. Anyone can start, but everyone won't finish. Reward comes to those who finish. How you finish is determined by how you prepare. Being a finisher isn't a class you take on line. To finish anything of any substance requires discipline, denial, determination, and discernment.

Four D's:

- **Discipline** - code of behavior
- **Denial** - sacrifice of wants
- **Determination** - firmness of purpose
- **Discernment** - perception of spiritual direction and understanding

You've got to stay disciplined with the behaviors that have you successful. Deny yourself of wants that will sabotage your deadlines, and stick to your pursuit! Most of all, discern your way through connections and partnerships as you get closer to finishing. Don't quit courageous woman, and remember skill is hardly ever the reason a person quits; often times it's the pressure that comes with and against you completing the task at hand. Be courageous and drive through every detour and all discord that presents itself before your path. Be strong in the Lord and finish what you started! I believe you are a starter and a finisher! Finishing is about bringing it to a close—to the final stage—or simply completing it! Courageous woman, bring it home. Whatever it is you're working on, bring it home.

Finishing is a mentality that's developed through daily discipline. Complete it like you dreamed it before your started it! Our key verse says, "Finishing is better than starting." Maybe you're reading this saying, "I didn't start the project that's in my hands," but you have been put into a unique position to be the finisher. Well finish and finish strong! Don't walk away until you can say boldly "It is finished!" Patience is better than pride so it's okay if people start to say you look like you're not going to finish! Let them talk! You're not trying to look like a finisher, you are finishing. Pride has nothing to do with your success, your faith does.

Some people are planted by the enemy just to frustrate your purpose, so stay patient in all delays. Patience is at work while you finish every detailed part like the finisher you are.

"So now finish the work you started. Then your 'doing' will be equal to your 'wanting to do.' Give from what you have. (2 Corinthians 8:11, New Century Version)

In this text, Paul is talking about offerings or giving, but take the principle and apply it to anything you've started and here what He's saying: when you finish what you start, your doing will be equal to your wanting to do. You normally want greatly to finish what's on your mind, now it's time to finish it in reality. Give from everything you have. Give your energy, attention, and your money. Finish!

Thank you, God, for courageous faith to finish all products, deals, programs, and projects that are in my hands and those of which my hands are a part. In Jesus' name. Amen.

Day 16

Start in faith. Stay in faith.

COURAGEOUS STARTER

"Is there anyone here who, planning to build a new house, doesn't first sit down and figure the cost so you'll know if you can complete it? [29] If you only get the foundation laid and then run out of money, you're going to look pretty foolish. [30] Everyone passing by will poke fun at you: 'He started something he couldn't finish.'"

(Luke 14:28-30, The Message)

Starter: a person who initiates or sets going, one that begins to engage in any activity or process.

Most people can't wait to get started! It's something about having new ideas, new concepts, and being motivated to begin. Many people are so eager to begin that they start without being ready to run after taking off. I'm talking about running in faith! Starting definitely matters; people say it doesn't matter how you start, just start. I disagree! Your start matters just don't procrastinate because of fearing the unknown. God didn't give you the spirit of fear so give it back! With all the free information available at the touch of a finger and revelation knowledge from God, starting should never begin in ignorance.

Starting of course involves more than surfing the World Wide Web and praying! It's more than having a strong desire and a great idea.

Make Sure You Start With:
- Courageous Faith
- Crazy Work Ethic
- Do Your Due Diligence
- Have Real Skill
- More Than Your Self (team)
- Vision

Start in faith and stay in faith! That is the advice I'm going to give you! Sit down and count up the cost! Finances aren't your only cost, and don't allow the cost to keep your start in dream status. Courageous woman, you will have to calculate the emotional, relational, financial, and the spiritual. Count up all of these, know what and where your lane is, and run your own race celebrating every step of your way.

In our key verse, the writer says "Make sure you count the cost before you start so finishing won't be an option." Most mistakes are made when we don't plan for them when starting. Understand my vernacular when I say mistakes—that's what I mean, not sin. Don't over spiritualize it. Sin is missing the mark. A mistake can be missing a meeting, misrepresentation of yourself, or simply miscommunication that could cost you. Be a courageous starter and go beyond just feeling good about starting to know it's all good. You are courageous and you have enough courageous faith to start. Faith isn't magic and it should push you into corresponding action. When you start anything you have to sit and plan. Your plans should be shared with people who have proven work to help advise you beyond your start.

"Plans fail without good advice, but they succeed with the advice of many others." (Proverbs 15:22, New Century Version) Having good advice will accelerate your plans and opportunities for success. Plans aren't everything. They aren't to take the place of God, but they do matter greatly. Goals without plans are wishes.

"May He give you what you want and make all your plans succeed." (Psalm 20:4, New Century Version) Start it and do it courageously!

Dear God, I thank you for starting power, many advisors, and I believe the plans you've given me are exactly what's needed to complete what's needed. In Jesus' name. Amen.

Day 17

You and your status is a gift from God.

COURAGEOUS SINGLES

"And the Lord God formed man of the dust of the ground, and breathed into his nostrils the breath of life; and man became a living soul."

(Genesis 2:7, King James Version)

Single: unmarried, not involved, one.

Paul tells us in **1 Corinthians 7:7: singleness is a gift.** Being single in the book of Corinthians is described as a gift. No matter how you feel about being single, make sure you line up with what the Word says about it. You're courageously gifted! Being single has its pros and cons, but so does everything else in your world. If you can use your faith for healing, money, houses, car, jobs, promotions, and other miracles, I don't see why you can't use your courageous faith for a spouse! Stay in the faith no matter what and believe you're never alone.

Adam was not only single for some time, but he was alone, I mean literally alone. He was the only human being. Let the thought of his single life soak in and then you can see to gift of singleness clearer. You are such a gift, single and courageous woman. When God made

Adam, he was single but he was whole, healthy, and honest. Adam was packaged with heaven's best! He was full of God and Eden was his home. He had dominion over everything on the Earth. He was the visible image of God in flesh. He was brilliant in that he named every species of animal and had no formal education. He had the spirit of God as his teacher! Adam was so driven that he himself never asked for a woman. God said it wasn't good for him to be alone.

After God said that, He sent all the animals to him to be named and Adam named them without an attitude. Think about how long this took and let it sink in that he didn't quit because of being lonely or disturbed because he had no one! Nope those verses aren't in the Bible! He was alone and God sent one gift to another gift! You are a gift, sister, and that's what the Word called you! No matter how you feel, remember that!

The characteristics of the first single person on the Earth from scripture (Adam):

- Whole
- Healthy
- Honest
- Had Dominion
- Visible Image of God in the Flesh
- Brilliant
- Full Of God
- Worked In The Garden (employed)

I believe these eight descriptions are wonderful characteristics surrounding Adam, who was single until Eve was formed from him for him. Every single, whether male or female, should recognize that these eight characteristics have been available since Eden. Courageous woman, yes, beauty is important, but I can tell you having all eight of these characteristics is very attractive to a man. They're courageous!

Don't compromise any of these if you start feel lonely. You and your status is a gift from God. God brought Eve to Adam! Yep, that's what I said! God made her from his rib, but she was brought to him. I know the scripture is often quoted, "He that finds a wife finds a good *thing,* And obtains favor from the Lord." This is true and it is the Word, but that doesn't mean the man won't find favor if he's found by you. You were handmade by God and you are heaven's best!

Remember Eve was called a helper. She was created because there was no helper suitable for him. Suitable means fit; she was the right fit for him. When Adam saw her, he called her bones of my bones and flesh of my flesh. God sent every creature of the Earth to him to name, so she had to follow the same order. God brought her to him and he called her woman. God made her, Adam named her, and she was made to what he needed. She possessed the Big Eight, because she came from it. This is vital while you're single! Adam was whole before he had Eve. You make sure you are what God made, not what you think a man wants you to be! Leave that up to God.

Eve was the help Adam needed. You want to be the help that's needed for marriage, not just his woman. You must help meet the needs of life, not just be overwhelmed with joy to have your needs met. Until then, my courageous sister, possess the **Big Eight** and be strong alone instead of being strung along! Lonely and alone are two different things!

I know it can be tough being single, but don't discount yourself because you're still off the shelf. Stay right there. Someone wants you. The moment you come off shelf because you decided to be half price, you'll regret it! One of the definitions of single is one. You owe it to yourself and future spouse to still be one—not in pieces when you give yourself to them. You are a courageous woman with courageous faith. If you want to stay single, stay single; but stay in faith!

Father, I thank you that I am a strong single and I possess the qualities of Adam. In Jesus' name. Amen.

Day 18

Queens are game changers. God chose you to be royal, courageous woman. Take your royalty by faith.

COURAGEOUS QUEENS

"When the queen of Sheba heard of Solomon's fame, which brought honor to the name of the LORD, she came to test him with hard questions."

(1 Kings 10:1, New Living Translation)

Queen: King's wife; female ruler; a woman regarded as excellent; the most powerful chess piece that is able to move any number of unobstructed squares in any direction along a rank, file, or diagonal on which it stands.

In the game of chess, the queen is the most powerful piece in the game and is able to move vertically, horizontally, and diagonally. She can move! I want to encourage you now to make moves today. You can change the momentum for everyone connected to you. One song writer said "When I move you move (just like that)." Just like that, queen, you can shift everything.

Courageous queens are wives, singles, divorcées, widows, orphans, and foster children. Neither your marital status, natural birth, certainly not circumstantial status, determine your queenship. God chose you to be a royal, courageous woman. Take your royalty by faith!

"But ye are a chosen generation, a royal priesthood, a holy nation, a peculiar people; that ye should shew forth the praises of him who hath called you out of darkness into his marvellous light." (1 Peter 2:9, King James Version)

You are a royal, courageous woman! All of you are daughters of God! Some of you are married to an earthly king (husband). All of you should be regarded as a woman of excellence! No matter the vantage point from which you're viewed, your royalty should be seen. Say to yourself out loud: "I am a courageous queen." You weren't chosen to be royal just for royalty's sake! Royalty is flowing from you in five main areas—authority, money, property, family, and strategy. Queen, be a catalyst for change. Whether you're married, single, with or without kids, it doesn't matter. Queens, just flow in your power and create ways for others today!

The Kings of Israel's wives didn't have ruling power, they just had the honor of the title denoting royalty! There is no more denoting royalty and certainly you're more than just a title! Flow, courageous woman.

You are like Queen Sheba! She was royalty, had honor, and ruling power! She was powerful enough to set a meeting with King Solomon to test him to see if he really had the wisdom like everyone said! She had her own sit down with power! The key verse says she tested him with hard questions. This statement reveals her level of intelligence and wisdom. She was smart, rich, and she was blessed enough to bless him! Rich and powerful not only sounds good, but they both belong to you.

"Your power is great, and your glory is seen everywhere in heaven and on earth. You are king of the entire world, [12] and you rule with strength and power. You make people rich and powerful and famous. [13] We thank you, our God, and praise you." (1 Chronicles 29:11-13, Contemporary English Version)

Courageous woman, his glory is also seen in you. God will make you rich, powerful, strong, and famous. His power is your source, queen. Get ready to sit with other powers in your city. You're about to birth something new for all the queens that haven't realized who they are yet!

You Are Courageous Queens.

Father, I thank you for royalty! I am royal because of who you are! I am a courageous queen and I'm blessed going in and coming out. In Jesus' name. Amen.

Day 19
Stay in command and keep Him in charge.

COURAGEOUS ENTREPRENEUR

Entrepreneur: a person who organizes and operates a business or businesses.

In charge: in control or with overall responsibility.

You've believed and worked yourself to prominence in your career! You have people reporting to you and you're responsible for them. You're high-powered, highly motivated, and driven from within! Some of you reading this may be saying to yourself, "Well I'm not there yet, so this isn't for me today." You are mistaken, and yes it is! We don't speak what we see, we speak what we want to see.

"Death and life is in the power of the tongue: and they that love it shall eat the fruit thereof." (Proverbs 18:21, King James Version)

You may not be the owner today. You might be a volunteer, receptionist, first, second, or third assistant. All of that can change with one ounce of faith and the favor of God and man. You can faith your way into supervision, management, partnership and ownership. Be courageous in your approach to advancement! The book of James tells us "Faith without works is dead." Work with faith where you are and not like you hate where you are. Hate and faith don't mix. Speak with courageous faith, woman of God. Ownership is a part of your life, and your days of working for someone else are coming to an end. You are about to start signing checks for someone else to enjoy life. You are not the borrower, you are the lender. You aren't beneath, you are the head!

There are four things I want to release to you:

1. "Put God in charge of your work, then what you've planned will take place." (**Proverbs 16:3, The Message**)

    You still have to plan and work! Faith isn't magic, so get that out of your head! You're going to have to work your business with passion! You are the owner, but put God in charge! If you keep God in the proper place of the business he gave you, he will always stay God and you won't look like your trying to become him. People don't knowingly try to be God; but when they keep God out after accomplishing greatly, some feel they no longer need him because they worked so hard get what they have. In general, people sometimes suffer from the power because they won't submit to power! Keep seeking him first before all business strategies, meetings, and deals! Your business deal is right on the other side of you committing your work to him. Stay in command and keep him in charge!

2. "Work brings profit, but mere talk leads to poverty!" (**Proverbs 14:23, New Living Translation**)

    I don't think its rocket science, by any means, that profit is necessary and wonderful for business. Profit is financial gain, especially the difference between the amount earned and the amount spent on merchandise and operating. Profit doesn't appear out of the sky. Work brings in profit. As you move into the season of working for yourself don't even think about being lazy! Work will bring profit, but talk leads to poverty! When a courageous woman speaks, she's speaking faith. She understands her world is framed by her words!

3. "The blessing of the LORD makes a person rich, and he adds no sorrow with it." (**Proverbs 10:22, New Living Translation**)

   As you continue in business, wealth is going start attaching itself to you like static; remember, it's the Blessing of the Lord! You can get rich through hard work, but God has a plan with your hard work that prohibits sorrow. The blessing is on your life. It's not there only for you to say I'm blessed, it's there to prosper you every day financially! You are courageously in charge and in command! Take control of your investments, own it, and get paid! It's time to be rich without the world's problems.

4. "For what shall it profit a man, if he shall gain the whole world, and lose his own soul?" (**Mark 8:36, King James Version**)

   Work your company right to the top, but don't get so deep that you work yourself right out of the will of God. If you start with courageous faith, make sure you stay with courageous faith. Why get all of the money, raise up your company, and lose your relationship with God?

Father, thank you for the mind to create new businesses and the power create wealth! The blessing is on me and its making me rich without sorrow. In Jesus' name. Amen.

Day 20
There will be no change where there
is no challenge.

COURAGEOUS HEALTH

"Training your body helps you in some ways, but serving God helps you in every way by bringing you blessings in this life and in the future life, too."

(1 Timothy 4:8, New Century Version)

Health: the state of being free from illness or injury, a person's mental, emotional, and spiritual condition.

There isn't one thing wrong with having courageous faith and a courageous body. It's time for you to be courageously healthy! What is courageously healthy? It is actively being free from sickness, staying in shape, and staying in faith. So often, women are strong in other areas and weak in this one. Many of you can pray heaven down, but can't put down unhealthy emotions and or bad foods. I want to encourage you to get fit in all three. Be fine and stay fine; have faith and stay in faith.

This is a new season of discipline for you. If you don't have a plan, get a plan (from a creditable source of course). If you have a plan, stick to the plan. If you're on a plan but there's not much challenge, switch things up and make it more intense! Take courage and attack your diet and training. Lazy, super-spiritual people love to discredit training the body because of how Timothy phrases the verse. He discusses the small value of it in comparison to serving God. When people hear the phrase "little value," they assume it has no value. This is far from the truth. You only have one body and the better you take care of it the better your life here on earth will be.

Have the courage to sign up for healthy challenges—attack them and finish them. There will be no change where there is no challenge. If you want to see a difference in your appearance, then you can't just appear in the gym. You have to bring effort to your appearance. The same applies to your inner man. If you don't act on the Word, you're only going to be a hearer of the word and not much will change for you. When you actually start doing it, challenges will come. Like the Bible says in **Philippians 4:13, "You can do all things through Christ because he strengthens you."**

Timothy is saying that training the body helps the body and that the body is temporary. That's why he says it's of little value. You can train the body, just don't ignore the other parts of your being. Your mind needs transformation and your spirit needs saving! All parts of you matter, courageous woman.

"Beloved, I pray that all may go well with you and that you may be in good health, as it goes well with your soul." **(3 John 1:2, English Standard Version)**

God wants us healthy and he wants things to go well for us. He wants us to prosper in the soul and the body. Your soul is your mind, will, imagination, and emotions; he wants all of that healthy too!

Serving God is how your soul and spirit will become fitter than ever. Your soul, spirit, and body matter to God, or he wouldn't have given them to you.

"Or do you not know that your body is a temple of the Holy Spirit within you, whom you have from God? You are not your own, [20] for you were bought with a price. So glorify God in your body." (1 Corinthians 6:19-20, English Standard Version)

Your body doesn't belong to you, so glorify God in it while you have it. God gave you the body you have and everything you do in it should bring him glory. Your body is the temple of the Holy Spirit

It's going to be very important that as you get the body you desire, your desire for him stays stronger. Don't allow your own wisdom to pull you away from the word. Faith comes from it.

"Don't be impressed with your own wisdom. Instead, fear the LORD and turn away from evil. [8] Then you will have healing for your body and strength for your bones." (Proverbs 3:7-8, New Living Translation)

Courageous faith won't take you away from the Word. As you reverence God, healing will always flow through your body. A courageous healthy life is one that's blessed in the here and now and forever more.

Father, I thank you for a healthy life. I am free from all sickness and disease. My mind, body, and spirit are in great shape. In Jesus' name. Amen.

Day 21
Financial freedom is a mindset...

COURAGEOUS PAY OFF

"She went and told the story to the man of God. He said, 'Go sell the oil and make good on your debts. Live, both you and your sons, on what's left.'"

(2 Kings 4:7, The Message)

Pay off: to eliminate debt, the final payment of a debt, to pay the complete amount.

Today, I want to encourage you to pay off something you owe. If you can't afford to pay it off out right, be proactive and start a plan. Don't just start it mentally, but put it in motion literally. Some of what I'm about to say won't make sense, but it will make faith. Yes there are many plans that work to eliminate debt and we've used them, but God also uses supernatural ways to pay off debt, as well. In the Old Testament, every seven years all debts were canceled because God said so! Bills, we cancel you now!

It always feels good to be able to purchase the things that you want. On the other hand, it's devastating not having the capital or credit to purchase what you need or desire. Your income and credit are key factors in being able to do so. Keep in mind, if a bank lends you money to purchase what you desire then it's agreeable that you can afford it. With that being said, paying the debt and becoming free of it should be part of your debt-free goals. Courageous woman, thirty-two years is a long time to pay for a home, five years is a long time to pay for a car, and two years is a long time to pay for furniture. Have courageous faith and believe God's truths for debt cancellation or a courageous pay off. Believe and back off from buying your wants to pay off debts.

Often times when God blesses financially, the desire to spend anticipates while the courage to pay off dissipates. If you give, God will give back to you. The question is: what are you going to do with what he gives back? (Pay off something.)

Debt isn't sin and that's nowhere in scripture. **"The rich rule over the poor, and the borrower is servant to the lender." (Proverbs 22:7, Amplified Bible, Classic Edition)** A season of your life is mortgaged. When you borrow, you are under the power of the lender. It's time for you to be the lender and no longer the borrower. You don't have to be rich to start lending. You can do that from where you are finically now! Financial freedom is a mind set and it will make life for you so much better! Are you willing to change how you live now so you can live how you want later? You are one change from the start of living financially free! In our key scripture, the Prophet Elijah told the woman to sell the oil in her home and make good on her debts. She obeyed! She had courageous faith and acted on the word. This was sparked by the supernatural and her obedience to the man of God.

The prophet told her to get all the jars she could collect from her neighbors and fill them up to the brim with oil. She said all she had was just a little oil; but because she moved in faith, that little oil multiplied and payed off her debts! Now, just think how she will see and speak about everything else she has or wants. No longer do you need to see what you have as it is, but see it like you want it to be. Not only were her debts paid, but she had enough left over to buy necessities. She had an overflow from a little! What kind of overflow will you live off of when you see what you have in faith? No longer will you have to live off what you have left. You're getting ready to live a life where money isn't an issue. It's time for you live. Your days of loans and high interest rates are over! Believe God, pay tithes, give cheerfully, sow bountifully and believe you can pay cash for what you need and want. I believe a pay off is here right now. Courageous woman, pay it off!

A Few Scriptural Reminders:

Romans 13:6-8, The Message

That's why you pay taxes—so an orderly way of life can be maintained. Fulfill your obligations as a citizen: pay your taxes, pay your bills, and respect your leaders. Don't run up debts, except for the huge debt of love you owe each other.

Proverbs 17:18, The Message

It's stupid to try to get something for nothing, or run up huge bills you can never pay.

Ecclesiastes 5:5, The Message

Vow it, then do it. Far better not to vow in the first place than to vow and not pay up.

Deuteronomy 15:1-3, The Message

At the end of every seventh year, cancel all debts. Everyone who has lent money to a neighbor writes it off. You must not press your neighbor or his brother for payment—all debts are canceled, according to God. You may collect payment from foreigners, but whatever you have lent to your fellow Israelite you must write off.

Father, I thank you for natural and supernatural pay offs now. In Jesus' name. Amen.

Day 22

Friendship hasn't been truly tested
until it has been challenged.

COURAGEOUS FRIENDSHIP

" Friends come and friends go, but a true friend sticks by you like family."

(Proverbs 18:24, The Message)

Friendship: state of mutual trust and support between people.

One of the greatest ships in the world is friendship! Friendship is about investing in the function of friendship. It›s about having friends that have friendship potential to keep the ship moving. This life was never meant to be lived alone. It was meant to be shared with others—to sharpen one another. If you live life alone, you do stay protected from the folly that happens in some friendships, but at the price of a lonely life. Many people have chosen the solo path to keep themselves from unnecessary drama and betrayal. The fear of betrayal and the personal experience of it has caused a lot of people to close themselves off from experiencing great friendships. I'm talking about real friends with mutual affection, not the casual term that is thrown around because you went out to eat together one night! I'm talking about a true investment from each other.

For some of you, it's going to take courageous faith to trust others. Trust is hard to reestablish once it's been violated, but be careful that you don't treat people like they've already violated your trust. Give people a chance before placing them on the "no friends list." Being open isn't being unaware. Give people a chance before you write them off. There are many forms of friendships, but all share the following characteristics: sympathy, empathy, honesty, compassion, trust, and the ability to express feelings.

Friendship hasn't been truly tested until it has been challenged. Be courageous when misunderstandings and miscommunication alter the ship you and your friends are on. Remember you get the relationships that you build! You get exactly what you build! Build debatable opportunities for you and your friends to agree to disagree and see how your friends handle disagreements and disappointments. A friendship that can't survive disagreements isn't worth supporting. Build everything into your true friendships. You get what you build!

"A friend loveth at all times, and a brother is born for adversity." **(Proverbs 17:17 King James Version)**

Real friends love at all times—the scripture confirms. All times means anytime and every time you or your friends decide to go another way. Friends love each other; they don't just like or put up with each other. This proverb says "A brother is born for adversity." When you really become friends, the relationship goes deeper than the surface. It reforms into family that sticks, and brothers and sisters are born from a real friendship!

Don't fear making friends, but know that the Word says they come and go but real friends stick like family! Your obligation for friendship is to show yourself friendly and then be what you show! Today, courageously invest in a friendship you are in but haven't put forth much effort . Don't walk in fear; walk in faith and in wisdom. You already know what bad company is so stay in the Word to discern the wolves in sheep clothing.

Friendship Keys From Scripture:

1 Corinthians 15:33, New Living Translation

Don't be fooled by those who say such things, for "bad company corrupts good character."

Proverbs 12:26, New Living Translation

The godly give good advice to their friends; the wicked lead them astray.

Proverbs 13:20, New Living Translation

Walk with the wise and become wise; associate with fools and get in trouble.

Proverbs 27:6, New Living Translation

Wounds from a sincere friend are better than many kisses from an enemy.

Proverbs 18:24, New Living Translation

There are "friends" who destroy each other, but a real friend sticks closer than a brother.

Father, I thank you for the wonderful friendships I have and the others that are on the way. In Jesus' name. Amen.

Day 23

Joy is an eternal possession.

COURAGEOUS JOY

"May the God of hope fill you with all joy and peace in believing, so that by the power of the Holy Spirit you may abound in hope."
(Romans 15:13, English Standard Version)

Joy: fruit of the spirit.

You can't pretend to have joy, but you can pretend to be happy. Joy will stay with you, even if you're going through a trying time. It is an eternal possession. Paul writes in **Galatians, Chapter 5**, revealing the fruit of the spirits as: love, joy, peace, patience, kindness goodness, faithfulness, gentleness and self-control. Joy is an eternal, immortal, internal power given to us by God to flow in daily. Happiness, however, is the result of something good happening to you or for you. It always needs a catalyst to manifest its sporadic or vacillating effects. By no means am I insinuating that I don't want you happy or that happiness is a bad thing! I want everyone in this world happy, but unfortunately everyone isn't going to get what they want when they're depending on someone or something to do it for them! Joy belongs to you.

"Always be joyful." (1 Thessalonians 5:16, Contemporary English Version)

Courageous woman, you're transitioning from waiting on something good to happen to be happy, to living in pure joy. Joy is associated with God, and happiness is associated with what happens for you. Joy is the result of God living in you. God already has this joy prepared to dwell in you not just happen to you. Live in joy, oh my God. In **James 1:2**, He tells us to count it all joy when we meet trials of various kinds. He says count it all joy when you meet trials of all kinds—not be unhappy, go into isolation, and be silent. Count what's happing to you as all joy. What a difference this makes in your perception of happiness. Be joyful no matter what!

"Be full of joy in the Lord always. I will say again, be full of joy. I love this Philippians verse because it tells us to be full of Joy always!" (Philippians 4:4, New Century Version)

In our key verse, Paul is saying God will fill you up with joy and fill you up with peace. Courageous woman, you're not having to depend on anyone to make you feel good, do well, or be happy. God is doing the filling so you can be at peace, be joyful at all times, and abound in hope. You're not hopeless and unhappy. No matter what you feel like God has never left you.

"When anxiety was great within me, your consolation brought me joy." (Psalm 94:19, New International Version)

You are full of the spirit and that is much, much broader than happiness. You're not living off of what happens to you, you're living from an eternal current that will keep you hopeful and courageous regardless of what's happening. You are full of joy, and the joy of the Lord is your strength! You are too strong to be weakened by what's not happening for you. Be courageous and flow from the joy that's within you. Joy is in you at an abounding capacity!

Father, I thank you for the courage to walk in joy and not wait on what happens to make me happy! I am so joyful that God has filled me with something better and joy is my better. In Jesus' name. Amen.

Day 24
There is a direct correlation between you and where your attention is.

COURAGEOUS FOCUS

"Don't shuffle along, eyes to the ground, absorbed with the things right in front of you. Look up, and be alert to what is going on around Christ---that's where the action is. See things from his perspective."

(Colossians 3:2, The Message)

Focus: the center of interest or the act of concentrating, central point of attention.

Focus is direct thinking. It's the ability to control and centralize your thoughts towards a specific area. Your focus is where your attention is, and to change your focus you must change what you've given your attention . It is harder doing it than it is saying it, but it can be done. As you begin, don't be surprised by all the head trash you hear and envision your adjustments. You will be at your best when you find the frequency needed for sustained momentum. This is a day to make some fine adjustments to your thought life.

"Be careful what you think, because your thoughts run your life." (Proverbs 4:23, New Century Version)

If you could draw all the thoughts from today on paper, you could view your focus outside of your mind. What would you see? There is a direct correlation between you and where your attention is. Though your focus is mental, it's revealed through your effort behind your actions. I want to encourage some of you to focus, some of you to refocus your focus, and some of you to stay focused. Every thought that has taken you away from the path, must be captured.

Your ability to focus clearly is critical for your advancement, so pray to protect your focus. The enemy wants to use your focus against you. You will find yourself concentrating in areas that aren't healthy, building stress, and worrying when you should be building your dreams. Courageous woman, take a look with your faith eye and see what the natural eye can't see. See where your attention has taken you and how high and far God has brought you!

Many of the decisions that you make from this time forward will reflect a renewed focus. Look up and be alert to what is going on around Christ—where the action is! Set your mind, set your focus, set your attention around Christ. No matter how the enemy tries to knock you off focus, stay set. As a matter of faith, sit in your set mind so that the enemy can see you rested in your focus. You now see everything from Christ's perspective!

Whatever you desire to be, have the courage to focus in faith on that matter. You cannot accomplish your goals if you won't make an extreme effort to focus. Success can be traced all the way back to your attention. Break every bad focus now, in the name of Jesus. Every fine detail that you haven't been able to produce is about to be born, because of your courageous faith. When you're told you can't do a thing, redirect your focus, don't have a pessimistic view, be optimistic in your head and mouth! Fight the good fight of faith and focus. Stay focused, especially when you begin to see layers of success coming to pass! Don't get comfortable and stop feeding your faith. Lock in even more, because it takes courageous faith to keep courageous focus!

Father, thank you for the ability to focus when I'm feeling good and when I feel like giving in. I am courageous and determined. In Jesus' name. Amen.

Day 25
Strength is for service.

COURAGEOUS STRENGTH

"I can do all things through Christ, because he gives me strength."
(Philippians 4:13, New Century Version)

Strength: state of being strong; the influence or power possessed by a person or organization.

You are the strongest creation on the Earth. God trusted you to carry the seed of man from generation to generation. He placed in you natural strength that survives life's most challenging times. Your strength serves mankind. The scriptures describe you as the weaker vessel, as in being compared to the natural genetic stature or vessel of man. Woman and man were created by the same matter, but for different purposes and positions. Man was made and you were fashioned; in other words, you were built. You were built with a helping nature.

"In the same way, you husbands should live with your wives in an understanding way, since they are weaker than you. But show them respect, because God gives them the same blessing he gives you-the grace that gives true life. Do this so that nothing will stop your prayers." (1 Peter 3:7, New Century Version)

Don't allow the word weaker to quantify your level of strength. You have the same grace in you and the same blessing on you. You are only called weaker than man when the two become one through marriage. Courageous woman, you are known for strength. Ironically, you're just weak enough to stop your husband's prayers from being answered.

That's pretty strong to me! It takes a strong woman to submit to another being, period; especially if that being in a marriage has the position of strength, but is actually weaker in wedlock! Submitting isn't weakness its strength's way of saying "I'm here to service you if and when you need me ."

Strength is for service. I don't care how many times you work out a week, your natural strength isn't strong enough to carry you through life. The strength you need comes from above. You have work to do for the kingdom, your family, and for yourself. The great thing about the work God has entrusted unto you: it doesn't require you to use your own power. Glory to God! In our key scriptures today, the text says "I can do all things through Christ that strengthens me."

You can! What an amazing word for you to receive. There are no ifs, ands, or buts about it. You can start the company! You can publish your work! You can invent the product! You can be the President! You can do all things through Christ that strengthens you. His power is serving you now as you read this. He is the source of your momentum. All things isn't just about what you think of, but even the things you have no clue of yet! Take courage right now and be strong in the Lord as you do all you want and need to do. His strength will help you go where you want and help you stay where you want. You've been given go power and staying power! You are going to need both for the adventure ahead of you. Stay courageously strong and trust in his

"He gives strength to those who are tired and more power to those who are weak." (**Isaiah 40:29, New Century Version**)

Tired in the natural brings more power from the supernatural! I told you, His strength is for service and it will work even when you feel weak.

But he said to me, 'My grace is enough for you. When you are weak, my power is made perfect in you.' So I am very happy to brag about my weaknesses. Then Christ's power can live in me. [10] For this reason I am happy when I have weaknesses, insults, hard times, sufferings, and all kinds of troubles for Christ. Because when I am weak, then I am truly strong." (**2 Corinthians 12:9-10, New Century Version**)

Courageous woman, you have courageous strength that works better when you submit yours to Him. Rest your strength and use His. You have an immeasurable supply of Christ's strength.

Father, I thank you providing me with an immeasurable level of strength for service. I give you glory and praise your name for supernatural power. In Jesus' name. Amen.

Day 26

Confession is faith's way of expressing itself.

COURAGEOUS CONFESSIONS

"That if thou shalt confess with thy mouth the Lord Jesus, and shalt believe in thine heart that God hath raised him from the dead, thou shalt be saved. [10] For with the heart man believes unto righteousness; and with the mouth confession is made unto salvation."

(Romans 10:9-10, King James Version)

Confession: an acknowledgement, it is the expression of a conviction of the heart.

Christianity is known as the great confession. You can't become a Christian without confessing Jesus with your mouth. It took courage for the followers of Jesus to confess him as savior. Christians were slaughtered for believing, and they didn't stop believing or confessing because of pressure. Pressure tries to choke your belief and change your confession.

"The seeds that fell among the thornbushes are also people who hear the message. [19] But they start worrying about the needs of this life. They are fooled by the desire to get rich and to have all kinds of other things. So the message gets choked out, and they never produce anything." (Mark 4:18-19, Contemporary English Version)

Remember, our confessions should agree with what the Word says, definitely not the opposite. There is no faith where there is no confession. Open your mouth and confess the word.

"Jesus answered, 'The Scriptures say: "No one can live only on food. People need every word that God has spoken.""" (Matthew 4:4, Contemporary English Version)

Your mouth is connected to your life. Confession, most of the time, takes on a negative meaning and is known as weakness, failure, sin, snitching, and guilt; but, my sister, confession is very positive and powerful. One of two mindsets are going to become your norm, depending on how you think and believe in your heart. This is vital because what you think and believe in your heart will affect your confession. Confession is faith's way of expressing itself. Your courageous faith starts with you believing in your heart, and, secondly, you speaking what you believe with your mouth. Your confession originates from your spirit man/inner man. Because faith is housed in your Spirit, you've got to speak words from your Spirit. Jesus said, in John 6:63 (New Living Translation), "The Spirit alone gives eternal life. Human effort accomplishes nothing. And the very words I have spoken to you are spirit and life." There is more to confession than just saying words. God's will for the words that come out your mouth (your confession) are to agree with His word. Your Confession should be an agreement between your belief and actions. Your agreement without your investment is an agreement that's nonexistent. Believe in what you say as much as you believe in what you see.

Be courageous, woman of God, and confess your way into destiny. Your courageous confession is how you access the promises of God. Confessions aren't made in your head, they're made from your mouth unto everything—salvation, healing, and prosperity! You can confess your way right into the next phase of your journey. Because your mouth is so critical to your success, make sure you watch it! Watch what you say! Don't talk yourself out of faith.

"Let no corrupt communication proceed out of your mouth, but that which is good to the use of edifying, that it may minister grace unto the hearers." **(Ephesians 4:29, King James Version)**

Corrupt communication, translated from the Greek, gives us these words: rotten, putrefied; worn out; of poor quality, bad, unfit for use, worthless."

Worthless conversation kills your confessions. Your everyday confessions are what set you up for ground breaking blessings! When your communication is worn out, your own heart is thrown into disarray and it causes you to question yourself! Stay courageous, woman of God, and keep your confession on the right side! Say what God says.

Father, I thank you and I praise you for giving me a way to access destiny by faith. I confess you as my Lord and only source. In Jesus' name. Amen.

Day 27
Don't limit your reality by being afraid to birth
what you see in your imagination.

COURAGEOUS IMAGINATION

"With God's power working in us, God can do much, much more than anything we can ask or imagine."

(Ephesians 3:20, New Century Version)

Imagination: images, the ability of the mind to be creative and resourceful forming new ideas and concepts.

Your imagination is a place that allows you to build anything, any way you like. There are no limitations in the world of your imagination, unless your reality is so rigid that you can't be abstract in your thinking. Your imagination is in you. The images that you see can fuel you or defeat you. There are movies playing in your head; pictures scrolling through your mind. Your soul is your mind, will, emotions, and imagination. I say that to inform you that you can have good soul ties. Every soul tie doesn't have to be bad. I want to encourage you to be tied to the new creative concepts flowing in your mind. There are millions of unearned dollars, several businesses, and witty inventions playing in your head that need to be brought out, processed, planned, and developed. All of this is working in your imagination and can manifest in your reality if you dedicate yourself to working it!

You can work it. Not only can you work it, but there is a power working in you that can go beyond your request and what you imagined. Research people who have already accomplished what you're seeing in your imagination. This will allow you to see it is already a reality for someone else. Interview them if you can, but if you can't, for some reason, then look for their stories through other forms of media to get the best insight you can. If there is no one available to interview, go to God, because you're going to have to seek him anyway. Never downplay God's view on your imagination. I believe mankind was formed from God's imagination, being made in his likeness and image. God is a spirit, but he had to have a blueprint in his head of what man would look like before he made him from dust. According to God's Word Translation, **Hebrews 11:3 says, "Faith convinces us that God created the world through His Word."** This means what can be seen was made by something that could not be seen. You can't see the imagination until it's birthed. Imagine, speak it, and believe it.

The scriptures says God can do much much more than you can even imagine. He can go beyond what you even ask. Don't limit your reality by being afraid to birth what you see in your imagination. Go into labor and push out those new creations. You will be pushing with a force stronger than you yourself can imagine. The key verse says, "Now unto him who is able to do above and beyond what you ask or think according to the power working in you." Jesus is already working, so work with him. The power working in you is unlimited in its nature, but yet limited to your revelation of it. Your revelation of the Word will help you fight the good fight of faith and bless your mind.

Courageous woman, use your imagination and don't just escape reality but instead use it to change your reality. The pathway to victory over anything that's been bothering you has an image attached to it.

The Word of God must be sown into your heart to replace the ineffective image with a Word-powered image. When you begin to not only hear the Word but see yourself as the Word, it says your imagination will become a nurturing place and not just fantasy zone. Imagine. Imagine. Imagine. Imagine. See what eyes haven't seen. Imagine yourself starting your company. Imagine yourself making the salary you desire. Imagine yourself purchasing your new home and car with cash. Imagine yourself having the man of your dreams! God has given you your imagination and His spirit to bring the unseen into reality! These two, working together, created the world and everything in it! Imagine. Imagine. Imagine. Imagine.

Father, I thank you for my imagination and the ability to bend things in my mind. Right now, I bring it into reality to change everything. In Jesus' name. Amen.

Day 28
Humanity is not frailty humanity
is God's creation

COURAGEOUS RELEASE

"In my distress I prayed to the LORD, and the LORD answered me and set me free."

(Psalm 118:5, New Living Translation)

Release: set free, remove restrictions, to make available; J-E-S-U-S.

Years ago, when I was a kid, we would sing a song in vacation bible school. The song asked the question, "How do you spell relief?" We would spell out the answer in song saying J-E-S-U-S! The world's answer for relief is a feeling of reassurance and relaxation following anxiety and distress. The song we sang as kids expressed Jesus as the better choice for believers than the world's definition. Receiving him brings relief.

"I give you peace, the kind of peace that only I can give. It isn't like the peace that this world can give. So don't be worried or afraid."
(John 14:27, Contemporary English Version)

"Are you tired? Worn out? Burned out on religion? Come to me. Get away with me and you'll recover your life. I'll show you how to take a real rest. [29] Walk with me and work with me---watch how I do it. Learn the unforced rhythms of grace. I won't lay anything heavy or ill-fitting on you. [30] Keep company with me and you'll learn to live freely and lightly." (**Matthew 11:28-30, The Message**)

Well, courageous woman, spell relief the same way: J-E-S-U-S.

The world says relief is to set free, remove restrictions, and to make available. The Word of God says, "He who the son sets free is free indeed!" Free indeed not just free! How do you spell release? J- E-S-U-S.With all this of being courageous I wanted to ensure you that it's ok to be strong and cry, Be strong and without worry, Be strong and be without stress, Strong and be angry. It's ok! It takes a lot of courage and faith to release your emotions. Doing so doesn't make you weak, it makes you human. Humanity is not frailty; humanity is God's creation.

"I said, 'You are "gods." You are all sons of God Most High.'" (Psalm 82:6, New Century Version)

You're not the Almighty God, but you are definitely the sons and daughters of God!

Courageous woman, can I tell you to please stop worrying and release yourself of the crippling effect it has on your humanity?

"Cast your cares on the Lord and he will sustain you; he will never let the righteous be shaken." (**Psalm 55:22, New International Version**)

Righteous woman, you were never meant to be shaken by anything from this Earth! God wants your cares and in return he's going to sustain you. Sustain means He's going to prolong your peace without interruption. Glory to God!

Say this out loud: "I am released now from anything that's causing me to worry, lose sleep, eat excessively, gain weight, . God I give you everything that's trespassing on me now!" **"The Spirit of the LORD**

is upon me, for he has anointed me to bring Good News to the poor. He has sent me to proclaim that captives will be released, that the blind will see, that the oppressed will be set free, [19] and that the time of the LORD's favor has come." (Luke 4:18-19, New Living Translation)

Jesus came to take from you what you keep holding on to! Take courage and let it go now!

"Don't worry about anything; instead, pray about everything. Tell God what you need, and thank him for all he has done. [7] Then you will experience God's peace, which exceeds anything we can understand. His peace will guard your hearts and minds as you live in Christ Jesus." **(Philippians 4:6-7, New Living Translation)**

Father, I thank you for the courage to let things go. I know I'm not weak because of how I feel, and I thank you for taking this weight now. In Jesus' name. Amen.

Day 29

What you do with your money today will
determine what your money will do
for you tomorrow.

COURAGEOUS MONEY MAKER

"Money that comes easily disappears quickly, but money that is gathered little by little will grow."

(Proverbs 13:11, New Century Version)

Money Maker: one that accumulates wealth, a lot of money.

The days of your money being spoken for before your payday comes are over. Living from check to check was never the plan God had for his people. Wealth belongs to you. You were not created to be poor, controlled by money, or live in poverty. Barely making it isn't who you are, either. Unfortunately, a lot of the statuses we label as poverty, were made from making poor financial choices. Poverty is a state of mind, a mental approach to life. It's not just having a low income. You can have a high income and have a impoverish state of mind. To those courageous women that are doing well financially, I applaud you, and I'm excited for you and your level of prosperity.

Show another courageous woman how **"a diligent hand can bring wealth and how a lazy hand makes poverty." (Proverbs 10:4)**

You will not be one of the women that are wealthy in financial currency and poor in kingdom currency. As you keep the kingdom before your desire to make more money, God will keep the heavens open.

"The LORD will open up his heavenly storehouse so that the skies send rain on your land at the right time, and he will bless everything you do. You will lend to other nations, but you will not need to borrow from them." (Deuteronomy 28:12, New Century Version)

God is going to bless everything you do and keep the blessing on your work.

God wants you to prosper and he has given you the power to create/make wealth. Courageous woman, you've been given **power** to make/create wealth.

"But you shall remember the LORD your God, for it is He who is giving you power to make wealth, that He may confirm Hi s covenant which He swore to your fathers, as it is this day." (Deuteronomy 8:18, New American Standard Bible)

"Wisdom is like money: they both help. But wisdom is better, because it can save whoever has it." (Ecclesiastes 7:12, New Century Version)

The wealthy mentality will value information about how to make more money, just as much as the money. Your mind and your money are about to meet and change the future of those to whom you're connected . Even after you've left this Earth, you will be leaving an inheritance not bill settlements. Your mentality of money is where the shift is about to take place; for some, it has already taken place. One thing is for sure, wishing is over and the reality of God's word for you is here. You have the power to create wealth.

Take action through biblical principles and business strategies and move into the next tax bracket. The more you make, the more you will give away. It's more of a blessing to give than it is to receive. What you do with your money today, will determine what your money will do for you tomorrow. Make it, tithe it, sow it, invest it, do all of these, as well as give some away. Be courageous, woman of God. I see you making more money through multiple streams on your journey to financial increase. No matter where you are financially, increase belongs to you!

First, remember God! No matter how much more money you make, if your mentality doesn't shift, you can make all the money you want and be in want. Give Him His and then let yours work for you. SecondHe is giving you power to create wealth! You don't have to shift jobs or even get a raise to make more. You can take what you have and make more happen with what you already possess. You have that kind of power. You are a courageous money maker with a wealthy mentality! Third, God is confirming his covenant by making sure you have access to His power for wealth. Think! Available to you right now, is a power that can change your money forever!

"By your wisdom and understanding You have acquired riches for yourself And have acquired gold and silver for your treasuries." (Ezekiel 28:4, New American Standard Bible)

The power is coming through the wisdom God provides. Your finances will change as soon as your mind changes! You are a courageous money maker with multiple incoming streams flowing. Your knowledge about money is about to increase and not because you wished it, but because you're going out to understand it. The key proverb in our daily reading says, "Money that comes easily disappears quickly, but money that is gathered little by little will grow." As you gather little by little, your wisdom will grow with it! As your wisdom grows, strategies will grow! Your money is about to accumulate multiple zeros. You will have a treasure; it's in your covenant! The blessing of the Lord makes you rich and adds no sorrow!

Father, I thank you for the power to create wealth and build it little by little! My mentality is not of poverty, but of one who is wealthy. I am a courageously making more money from new multiple streams. In Jesus' name. Amen.

Day 30

Giving is a matter of the heart.

COURAGEOUS GIVING

"Give, and you will receive. Your gift will return to you in full—pressed down, shaken together to make room for more, running over, and poured into your lap. The amount you give will determine the amount you get back."

(Luke 6:38, New Living Translation)

Give: freely transfer the possession something over.

The Bible says, "For God so loved the world he gave his only son." Calm down; that is not required of you! You don't have to give your only child. It almost seems that is how some people view the offering when you scan some auditoriums during the moment of giving. God freely transferred Jesus to the Earth to take care of man's sin problem. Courageous woman, you are the catalyst for other women to see you freely transfer wealth into the kingdom, without speculation and with gladness! Giving to God, the poor, charities, and other worthy causes keep you living with an open hand! Tight fists are for fighting, and they're a sign that you're fighting God's way to support ministry, prosper yourself, and your household. Courageous givers are beyond this kind of fight. Courageous givers give so much that worry might hit their mind, for a split second, thinking that they've given too much! That is how the natural mind thinks, and it makes every bit of sense, but we're here to make faith not sense.

"Sinners are always wanting what they don't have; the God-loyal are always giving what they do have." (Proverbs 21:26, The Message)

Courageous woman, you are a God loyalist and loyalists remain strong in the face of revolts. Remain faithful to honoring God with your substance. Giving to God isn't popular in certain circles within the church today. Be courageous with your giving right in the face of the non-givers who continue to show up to receive spiritual, but not financial, support.

I find it interesting that when Jesus did go in the temple, he was around the money watching. In Matthew 21:12-13, he's turning over the money changers tables and whopping them out the temple saying **"This house is a house of prayer, but you've made it into a den of thieves."** He also was in the temple watching people give. "Sitting across from the offering box, he was observing how the crowd tossed money in for the collection. Many of the rich were making large contributions. One poor widow came up and put in two small coins---a measly two cents. Jesus called his disciples over and said, **'The truth is that this poor widow gave more to the collection than all the others put together. All the others gave what they'll never miss; she gave extravagantly what she couldn't afford---she gave her all.'"** (Mark 12:41-44, The Message)

Gods not asking for all you have; he's asking for your heart. Your giving is a clear indicator of what he means to you. Everyone on earth finds a way to support who and what they love. Giving is a matter of the heart. The work of the kingdom on the Earth needs heart money to move not tip money.

Three Quick Courageous Giving Keys:

- Give equally of what you have, not what you think the kingdom should have.
- Give in faith, believing God for the supernatural promises attached to your obedience.
- Don't hold back our gifts because you may be struggling financially. He will supply all your needs according to his riches not yours.

My sister, giving is your key to being a kingdom distributor. You're going from just paying tithes, to giving offerings weekly, to sowing seeds, to always giving cheerfully, to giving jobs, giving to communities, and giving to other smaller companies. Courageous giving has no ending. Your gift will return to you in full—pressed down and shaken together—to make room for more—running over and poured into your lap. The amount you give will determine the amount you get back.

There is a return coming and it's coming with heaven's assistance, so more can keep coming. The only thing that can stop it, is you ceasing your giving or you falling in love with your money.

Father, I thank you for the mind to give and the support of your kingdom here on the Earth! I am a courageous giver. In Jesus' name. Amen.

Day 31
Be You!

COURAGEOUSLY YOU

"You made my whole being; you formed me in my mother's body. I praise you because you made me in an amazing and wonderful way. What you have done is wonderful. I know this very well. You saw my bones being formed as I took shape in my mother's body. When I was put together there, you saw my body as it was formed. All the days planned for me were written in your book before I was one day old."

(Psalm 139:13-16, New Century Version)

Be You: "Be who you are, not who the world wants you to be." - Unknown Author

Courageous woman, be you! By no means am I insinuating that you've been faking. I want to encourage you to be all of what God has given you. Stop hiding your uniqueness that sets you a part from every other woman in the universe. Expose the masterpiece that he took time to handcraft in the dark for nine months. There is way more to you than your nine-to-five appearance and your church appearance! Show it! Some of you that have stress or uneasiness have it because you're the guard *and* the prisoner that's chained up! Let her loose. I'm not talking about attitudes and sin that's been dealt with by Jesus and the cross! I'm talking to saved, courageous women, not the counterfeit women—so back off, Devil! Let her loose! I'm talking about the "you" who is different, not the "you" you've created—the hero you wear to work, church, and everywhere else so you don't offend anyone. No more being uncomfortable for people who don't like you or could care less for you anyway!

Be You! Wear your hair the way you want ; wear the clothes you want ; drive what you want ; stop changing the way you talk; work your style. Styles that people don't understand are labeled as crazy and special! It's okay, be you. The world needs what God made or he wouldn't have taken the time to make you! Someone is looking for the "you" that God made, right now. Will they find you or what you created? There is a possibility that what you're so busy trying to be, God has already rejected it. Be You.

"But the LORD said to Samuel, 'Don't judge by his appearance or height, for I have rejected him. The LORD doesn't see things the way you see them. People judge by outward appearance, but the LORD looks at the heart.'" (1 Samuel 16:7, New Living Translation)

People judge what they can't understand. Let them judge. They will judge you regardless. **"God has made us what we are. In Christ Jesus, God made us to do good works, which God planned in advance for us to live our lives doing." (Ephesians 2:10, New Century Version)**

Allow your heart to come out in your life. Stop hiding it and Be You. God made you who you are! Not only did he make you who you are, but Ephesians says God made you to do good works. People may not understand you, but they will understand your work. Oscar Wilde wrote, "Be yourself; everyone else is already taken."

Now, let me clear so we have an understanding. Being you is the regenerated you not the unsaved you! Leave her where you left her when you received Jesus. You are a new race now. Be the born again you.

Take Some Advice From The Word:

"Do you think I am trying to make people accept me? No, God is the One I am trying to please. Am I trying to please people? If I still wanted to please people, I would not be a servant of Christ." (Galatians 1:10, New Century Version)

Key - Servant Of Christ - Be You courageous woman

Thank you, father, for creating me and molding me. I am fearfully and wonderfully made, and I'm courageous enough to show it. In Jesus' name. Amen.

ABOUT THE AUTHOR

Joel A. Tudman is a visionary, leader, husband, father, coach, and author. He is the founder and senior pastor of THENETCHURCH. TV in Oklahoma City, OK. Joel is a native of Mount Pleasant, Texas and attended Texas A&M Commerce and received a bachelor degree in sports studies in health (BS) and master in health with a minor in counseling. Joel has been preaching for 18 years and pastored his first church in Mount Pleasant, TX.

February 2005, he was hired by Oklahoma State University to join the Strength and Conditioning staff and started as a general strength and conditioning coach working with the football team. Within two months he was promoted to football team chaplain and life skills development/leadership coach. The objectives of the life skill/leadership sessions are to teach the football players how to lead among their peers and in difficult situations. Joel has a passion to reach male college and professional athletes because of the obstacles and challenges that he has experienced personally. He has been extremely effective and transformed the lives of many athletes and remains a mentor to some of the former players and some whom are now in the national football league.

In 2006, while at Oklahoma State University, he began a campus ministry hosting mid-week bible study services with college students. In 2008, Joel founded THENETCHURCH.TV with 10 young college students. The ministry was founded on the scripture Matthew 13:47 (NIV) *"Again, the kingdom of heaven is like a dragnet cast into the sea, and gather fish of every kind."* The vision of the ministry is to have individuals come from all walks of life (e.g. the church and the un-churched).

Since the churches inception, the ministry has given to the community through different outreach initiatives including Christmas in November, free gas give-a-ways, serving inmates in corrections facilities on Thanksgiving Day, turkey give-a-ways, and hosting a college fair for inner city high school students. Joel's number one passion is preaching and teaching about Jesus Christ to reach his generation bridging the gap between new and old.

He lives in Oklahoma City with his wife, LaTasha Tudman and children and continues to transform Oklahoma City with his leadership and ministry outreach efforts.

www.ingramcontent.com/pod-product-compliance
Lightning Source LLC
LaVergne TN
LVHW021352080426
835508LV00020B/2245